Hurt

A CHERRYTREE BOOK

This edition first published in 2007
by Cherrytree Books, part of
The Evans Publishing Group Limited
2A Portman Mansions
Chiltern St
London
W1U 6NR

Printed in Malaysia

British Library Cataloguing in Publication Data

Amos, Janine
Hurt. - 2nd ed. - (Feelings)
1. Pain - Juvenile literature 2. Suffering - Juvenile literature
I. Title
155.4'124

ISBN 978 184234482 8
First published in paperback1997

CREDITS
Editor: Louise John
Designer: D. R. ink
Production: Jenny Mulvanny

VISIT OUR WEBSITE
www.evansbooks.co.uk
Evans

Hurt

By Janine Amos
Illustrated by Gwen Green

CHERRYTREE BOOKS

Billy's story

Hometime! The children dashed out into the playground.

"There he goes – Little Bill!" shouted some boys from Billy's class. Billy kept his head down. He pretended that he couldn't hear.

"Hey, Billy!" called another boy. "What's it like down there, shortie?" The other boys sniggered.

As usual, Billy felt his eyes fill with tears. He went red. As the teasing went on, he felt worse and worse. Then Billy turned and shouted at the boys.

"Leave me alone! I hate you!" Billy started to run. He wished he wasn't the smallest boy in the class.

At home Billy burst through the front door and slammed it behind him. He didn't want to see anyone, so he made for his room.

"Hi, Billy!" called his dad. "Come here a minute." Billy went into the kitchen. He pulled off his school bag and sent it skidding across the floor.

Why didn't Billy want to see anyone when he got home?

"I hate being small," said Billy crossly, and he told his dad all about the teasing.

"I know exactly how you feel," said Billy's dad when Billy had finished. "I was the shortest boy in my class when I was at school." Billy was surprised. He'd never thought of his dad as being small before.

Then Billy's mum came into the kitchen. She went over to Billy's dad and gave him a kiss.

"I like you being small," she said. She smiled at Billy. "What silly names do these teasers give you then? Let me guess. Titch?"

"Yes," said Billy.

"Shortie?" guessed Billy's dad.

"That's right," said Billy.

"Squirt?" asked his mum, giggling.

"Yes," laughed Billy, "and tadpole."

"Tadpole?" shouted Billy's mum and dad together. "That must be the silliest!"

The next morning Billy met the teasers again.

"Here comes Titch!" they called. But this time Billy didn't put his head down. He didn't feel like crying, and he didn't run away. Instead Billy remembered laughing with his mum and dad.

"Titch is a silly name," he thought, "but not half as funny as tadpole!"

How did Billy's mum and dad help?
Who would help you if you were feeling hurt?

Feeling like Billy

Have you ever been teased, like Billy? If you have, you'll know how much it hurts. Most people are teased at some time or another. It's especially hard when you're teased about something you can't change, as Billy was.

Don't help teasers

Some people think it is fun to hurt others. They like to see someone go red and get upset. If you're being teased, try not to show what you are feeling. Then the teasers might give up. Don't let the teasers know that you care.

Talking about it

If you're feeling like Billy, tell someone. Talk to someone you trust. Like Billy and his parents, you could talk about the silly words that teasers use. Together you could think up some answers to give the teasers next time. Think of things to say that show you don't care.

Think about it

Read the stories in this book. Think about the people in the stories. Do you ever feel like them? Next time you feel hurt, ask yourself some questions. What can I do to help myself? Who can I talk to? Then find someone you trust – a teacher, a parent or a friend. Tell them how you're feeling, just as Billy did.

Annie's Story

Annie sat in front of the television. She wasn't really watching the programme, but it was something to do.

"Come and tell me about your day at school, Annie!" called her mum from the kitchen. Her mum was getting tea ready and Annie knew that she should be helping. But Annie didn't want to talk. Nothing was the same since her dad had left home.

Annie heard her brother Matthew coming in from school. She liked Matthew but he was getting on her nerves these days. He was always trying to make her laugh – or talk about Dad.

"Hi there, funnybones!" said Matthew, sitting down next to Annie. "What's this programme about?"

"Shh!" snapped Annie. She didn't want to talk to Matthew either.

 Why do you think Annie doesn't want to talk?

At teatime Annie was very quiet. She knew that her dad was coming later. Every Friday evening he collected Annie and Matthew for the weekend. They stayed with their dad in his new flat, and he took them somewhere special as a treat.

"Have you packed yet, Annie?" asked her mum.
"I'm not going," said Annie.
"But you've been before," said Annie's mum.
"Well, I'm not going now," replied Annie.
Annie's mum sent her upstairs to pack.

"You'll like it when you get there," said Matthew. "We always have fun at Dad's."

"Oh, you don't understand anything!" shouted Annie. Matthew went red.

"He's my dad too, you know," he said.

Why doesn't Annie want to go to her dad's?
How do you think she feels?

When Annie's dad arrived he gave her a big hug. Annie tried hard not to hug him back.

"What shall we do this weekend, Annie?" asked Annie's dad. "It's your turn to choose."

"Nothing," said Annie.

The next day Annie and Matthew drove into the countryside with their dad. When they had parked, Matthew and Annie ran round to the back of the car. They watched their dad take out two huge kites. Matthew's was red with a dragon and Annie's was blue and yellow with a long tail. Matthew was excited.

"Thanks, Dad!" he shouted. "Can we fly them now?"

"Yes," said his dad. "The wind's just right. I'll show you how to get them going."

Annie followed behind, dragging her kite along the ground.

Soon Matthew had learned how to let the wind lift his kite high into the sky.

"Shall we get yours going, Annie?" asked her dad.

"No thanks," said Annie.

"Well, don't drag it like that – it might rip," he warned.

"Good," said Annie quietly.

At the top of the hill Annie sat down. She could see Matthew in the distance, flying his red kite.

"Don't you like your present?" asked Annie's dad. He sat down next to her. Annie was feeling cross and sad at the same time, but mostly she felt like crying.

"You're cross with me, aren't you?" said her dad.

How do you think Annie's dad is feeling?

Annie's dad went on talking.

"I know I've hurt you by leaving home, Annie. I'm so sorry. I miss being with you and Matthew every day."

"You'll never come back home to live, will you?" asked Annie.

"No," said her dad. "But we'll see each other every week. I'll make sure of that."

"Being hurt feels awful," said Annie.

"I know," said her dad. "Your mum and I hurt each other – and now we're hurting you."

"It feels better when you talk about it though," said Annie.

When Annie got into bed that night she gave her dad a big kiss.
"I forgot to thank you for my kite," she said.
"You liked it really, then?" asked Annie's dad.
"Kites are lovely," said Annie, "but talking is better."

 How do you think Annie feels now?

Feeling like Annie

Have you been hurt, like Annie? If someone you love goes away, it hurts very much. You know it's not your fault, but that doesn't change things. Sometimes it's hard to understand adults and the things they do.

It helps to talk

Talking can help you to feel better. But talking isn't easy when you're very upset, and there's so much to say. But, as Annie found out, it is a good idea to share your feelings. Try talking to someone you trust. It helps.

Jerry's story

Jerry was eating his breakfast. It seemed to be taking a long time this morning, and Jerry was in a hurry. He was going skateboarding with his friend Mark.

Jerry was a whole year younger than Mark, but he was almost as fast on his skateboard. Jerry gobbled up the last of his cornflakes. Then he took a big mouthful of orange juice.

"Hey!" said Jerry's dad. "Where's the fire? What's the big rush?"

"I'm meeting Mark on the corner at nine o'clock," said Jerry. "I mustn't be late."

When Jerry got to the corner of the road he was five minutes early. He sat down to wait for Mark.

Jerry watched an old lady feeding some pigeons. He practised balancing on his skateboard. Then Jerry counted six red cars at the traffic lights. He watched a line of ants running through the cracks in the pavement.

Jerry waited for a long time. But Mark didn't come.

What would you do if you were Jerry?

At last Jerry walked to Mark's house. He peeped through the window. Was Mark still in bed? Jerry rang the doorbell.

"Hello Jerry," said Mark's mum. "Mark's not here. He's gone to the skateboard park."

"Oh," said Jerry.

Jerry walked to the park on his own. He was upset. Jerry was sure he'd been on time. Why had Mark gone without him? What had Jerry done wrong? Jerry didn't understand.

At the park, Jerry saw Mark with some other boys. Slowly Jerry went over to him.

"I've been waiting for you on the corner," said Jerry. "Did you forget?"

"No," said Mark, standing on his skateboard. "I knew you'd turn up. Watch me Ollie!"

How would you feel now if you were Jerry?

Jerry went round the circuit a few times. But he didn't feel like playing any more.

"I'm going to see my grandad," he called. "'Bye!"

But no one heard him.

Jerry's grandad lived in the next street. He was always pleased to see Jerry. Soon Jerry was eating biscuits and drinking a big mug of milk. Jerry told his grandad about Mark.

"So you're feeling hurt?" said his grandad when Jerry had finished. Jerry nodded.

"I agree that Mark should have waited for you," said Jerry's grandad.

"He promised!" said Jerry.

"But listen," said Jerry's grandad. "I bet Mark didn't mean to be unkind."

"He thinks I'm too young to play with him," said Jerry.

"No he doesn't," said Jerry's grandad. "You're making that up. I expect Mark was just in too much of a hurry. Now go on back to that park and have some fun."

Jerry felt much better after talking to his grandad. He carried his skateboard back to the park. Mark and the others were still there. Jerry stood and watched for a while. Then Mark saw him.

"Hey! Jerry!" shouted Mark. "Come and play!"

Jerry ran to join his friend. "Grandad's right again," he thought, smiling.

How did Jerry's grandad help?
Do you have someone to talk to when you're feeling hurt?

Feeling like Jerry

Sometimes people hurt us without meaning to. Mark didn't keep his promise to Jerry. That wasn't very kind of him. But Mark didn't mean to hurt Jerry. If you're feeling hurt, ask yourself a question. Did the person mean to upset me? You might find that the person didn't mean to be unkind –and that helps.

Feeling bad

Sometimes being hurt makes us feel bad about ourselves. When someone's hurt us, we may think we've somehow deserved it. Try not to think like this. No one deserves to be hurt.

Feeling good

When you're upset it helps to be with someone you know well. That's why Jerry went to see his grandad. If you feel bad, spend some time with a friend – until you're feeling good again.

Feeling hurt

Think about the stories in this book. Billy, Annie and Jerry were each hurt in different ways, and they each found someone to help them. If you're hurt, talking about it will help you, too.

If you are feeling frightened or unhappy, don't keep it to yourself. Talk to an adult you can trust, like a parent or a teacher. If you feel really alone, you could telephone one of these offices. Remember, there is always someone who can help.

ChildLine
Freephone 0800 1111

The Line
ChildLine helpline for young people living away from home
Freephone 0800 884444
3.30pm to 9.30pm (weekdays)
2pm to 8pm (weekends)

NSPCC Child Protection Line
Phone 0808 800 5000

The Samaritans
Phone 08457 909090